Exquisite Heats

CHERRYL FLOYD-MILLER is an American poet, playwright and fiber artist. A native of the Carolinas, she is noted for exploring cultural and feminine themes through folklore and sound devices. She has written two previous volumes of poems, *Utterance: A Museology of Kin* and *Chops*, which won a 2005 AIGA Gold SEED Award. Her work has appeared in numerous literary journals and anthologies, including *Poetry*, *Crab Orchard Review*, *Poemeleon*, *Terminus* and *MiPoesias*. A grant/fellowship recipient of Poets & Writers, Inc., Caldera, Idyllwild Summer in Poetry, Cave Canem, the Indiana Arts Commission and the Vermont Studio Center, she is a freelance writer and teaches independent writing courses in her community.

Also by Cherryl Floyd-Miller

POETRY
Utterance: A Museology of Kin
Chops

Exquisite Heats

CHERRYL FLOYD-MILLER

CAMBRIDGE

PUBLISHED BY SALT PUBLISHING
14a High Street, Fulbourn, Cambridge CB21 5DH United Kingdom

© Cherryl Floyd-Miller, 2008

Salt Publishing 2008

Printed and bound in the United States by Lightning Source Inc

Typeset in Swift 9.5 / 13

ISBN 978 1 84771 311 0 paperback

Salt Publishing Ltd gratefully acknowledges
the financial assistance of Arts Council England

1 3 5 7 9 8 6 4 2

For "Zeke," the original "Voodoo Chicken"

For Nile and Hannibal: Here are the instructions — how and how not to love . . .

Contents

Acknowledgements

The following poems appear in various literary journals, some in slightly different incarnations:

"Voice Lesson from Eleanora Fagan" appears in the Spring 2008 issue of *Amistad / Ars Poetica*.

"Burgeon" appears in Volume II, Issue 2 (2007) of *Poemeleon, The Prose Poem Issue*.

"Childless, An Abridged Blues" and "Fall of the House of Dora" appear in the 2007 No. 39 issue of *Pembroke Magazine*.

"Say-So" appears in the Summer 2007 issue of *Pluck! The Journal of Affrilachian Art & Culture*.

"Super Freak," "The Beautiful, Needful Thing" and "News of the weird: Penis roams MARTA train" appear in both audio and print format in the "Quest" 2007 issue of *MiPOesias*, guest edited by Evie Shockley. "Super Freak" was also performed on the BFC's "Spoken" program hosted by Jessica care Moore-Poole in 2005.

"Clay" also appears in the anthology *The Ringing Ear: Black Poets Lean South*, University of Georgia Press, March 2007.

"Is" appears in the 2006 anthology *Gathering Ground: A Cave Canem 10th Anniversary Reader*, February 2006.

"Snake Oil" and "Voodoo Chicken" won the 2006 Poetry Daily-Virginia Arts of the Book Companion Poems Contest. Both poems were published on the Poetry Daily website.

"Afterspotting" appears in the *Java Monkey Speaks Anthology*, Volume II, June 2006. "Afterspotting" also appears in the anthology, *Temba Tupu! (Walking Naked): The Africana Woman's Poetic Self Portrait*. (The Africa World Press, 2008).

"There Is No Other Phrasing for Ashy" appears in the *Java Monkey Speaks Anthology, Volume I*, June 2005.

"In Another Life: A Bluesman" appears in *Terminus*, Summer/Fall 2005.

"Clearance" appears in *Broad River Review*, Fall 2005.

"Otherness" and "Gray: 1981" appear in *storySouth*, Spring/Summer 2004. "Otherness" also appears in *Letters to the World : A WOMPO Anthology*, Red Hen Press, February 2008.

"Burnt Cork Bop" and "Clay" appear in the Fall 2004 issue of the *North Carolina Literary Review*.

"Trapeze: The Greatest Show on Earth" appeared in the Winter 2003 issue of *Warpland* and was the winner of the 2002 Hughes, Diop, Knight Poetry Award.

"Weaned: Breaking the Habit of Pork" appears in the Fall 2003 issue of *Crab Orchard Review*.

"Something called a wife beater" appears in the Spring 2003 issue of *sidereality*.

"Defecting: A Bop for Exit Signs," "Celie in Atlanta," and "Orange" appear in *The Southern Hum*, Fall 2005.

"Rhythm Method" appears in *Poetry Midwest*, Fall 2003.

Several of the poems in this collection were created in workshops led by Cecilia Woloch, Natasha Tretheway and Richard Garcia privately and during Idyllwild Summer in Poetry or during the poet's time as a DIALOG Fellow for the Fulton County Arts Council in Atlanta.

Special thanks to Collin Kelley, James Richardson, Jr., Allen Robinson, II and to the great *secret* voices of NefroDada for being sharp first readers and listening to early drafts.

Part One

It is just like fire; fire can heat your house or burn it down.

— FRANK LUNTZ

Trapeze: The Greatest Show on Earth

ONE.

A day of circus. My brother and I shimmy & jive in back seats
under the cream leather roof of our bay brown family
thunderbird. For five hard-earned dollars, we will get life-size
posters of midget twins in tuxedos, drum rolls & a ringmaster.
Lions & cheetahs crawl from immense steel play pens and I don't blink.
We, a black family from a shabby house, have rubbed two nickels
together for change. Even the flying Wallendas can't hang and connect
from our trapezes.

TWO.

We are a three-ring family flying our car bird to Richmond. We want circus.
Daddy peels a five-dollar bill from his wad of ones so we can see clowns,
painted men who look like bright nosegays—pinks, reds, oranges, white
and jumping yellows. Daddy's face is many browns and frowns. I look at him
looking at clowns, sucking popcorn husk from his teeth, same enamel suck
      noise
of the tongue as it slides over bicuspids making mouth wind after meat.
In an end ring, 22 clowns have begun to stow themselves in a chartreuse
Volkswagen bug. I remember that we have come to this tent riding the hum
of nut brown metallic roar and dreams. Beneath an alabaster cowhide roof,
      amid
knocking pistons, we are flowers, larkspurs blooming in daddy's yucca blades.

THREE.

The hucksters. Peddling peculiar to 5,000 natural curiosities.
In frenetic dramas, they've got our little red wagons:
Gen. Tom Thumb's thick minikin thighs scoot & ski
past ropedancers, tumblers; Gunther the Trainer cracks
the whip, leads the leopards tawny and black spots to jump
through fire. The one-trick pony simply gallops, nothing more.
Cud-chewing llamas raise their necks peeking us. We are a caravan
dressed in glimmer and dust, black people with pocket change.
We stagger in wide-eyed applause.

FOUR.

We are wire walkers. A black family from a threadbare house. Our own.
We have saved months of candy money for carnival. An enclosed car
of traveling talents, we entertain spectators, give a series of farcical
acts that end in faith. The greatest of these is putting *one day* and *soon*
in the same sentence. We survive falls. Plunge thousands of feet into straw.
Nothing is there to catch us.

Feng Shui

All my life, we've been
a single shot gun house,
a front and back door aligned.

Where I've entered worlds through you
(as a firstborn notmyfathersson woman),
we've chased the idea of the hug
around straight-edged corners
in affectionate rooms.

First yin you taught me, Mama,
was to throw away everything
you don't love—

starting with love.

Don't say it. Show it, don't say it.

A meridian between mother
and daughter divides.

Even now as I hear you
telephone the words
into me long distance,

I'm removing all the mirrors
from these walls.

Gray: 1981

for JVK (12.16.00–7.16.03)

A.

In the small, private eon after the gun goes off, I check
to see if we are dead, if the burden of bodies huddled in my bed
is bloody, insides out. The bullet has missed us all —
baby brother beneath the covers clasped below my ribs,
another brother fastened around my neck,
Mama, knife in hand, crouched near the footboard,
and me, screaming. Above the heartbeat in my throat,
and the creaking mattress coils, I am the lead noise
in the night. We are waiting for the footsteps in the hallway
to get to us.

B.

I imagine how we will look on the front page
next to the missing Atlanta children. Know our names
will stretch out beneath black headlines and taut white smiles.
We could be remembered as *happy* and *well-fed*. As *Smart,*
Our Boy, and *The Baby* — In that order. As *She Worked Hard*
For Her Kids. As *What Was Wrong With Him?* The world
would begin to identify us through the half-unknowing anecdotes
of John Aruja or Alice Pierce, by the dusty path we walk
each morning to the row of mailboxes on Carolina Rest Home
Road. In order to catch a yellow bus to school. *Edward Hope*
Smith, Alfred Evans, Angel Lenair, Milton Harvey, Yusef Bell . . .
We could be among those names. *Cherryl, Toby, Chadric*
and Vivian Floyd. And Wallace, the distraught husband, my father,
who might send our bodies plunging, afterwards, a splash
from the Gaston river bridge.

C.

I smell smoke. The roof of my mouth burns with tears. His footfall
reaches the door to my room. The knob turns. The shadow,
my father (who does not smoke) walks into my scream. Diffuses it.
Where is the gun? A cig hangs from his face. I can make out
the dimpled embers near his mouth. Ash. My eyes are swimming
in the smoky corona of light.

Is

1.

In *Glyph*, the mind of Percival Everett's Baby Ralph asks, "Is a photograph always present tense?" As in here I *am*! There you *are*! This *is* us as we are about to . . . as if it hasn't happened. As if we don't know our lives before and after the *is*.

2.

be: show: occupy space: go or come: equal in identity: signify: belong: exist: remain undisturbed or untouched

In a flash, it all *is*. We are all *is*.

3.

G.E.P. & Gio (separate is's) won't
permit picture takers to take them.
Steals part of the soul, they say.
But I am sneaky, eye them anyway,
eye their I's for soul, take away
their heats, preserve them in retina,
slip them onto films of *was* until I speak
them again. now, here I am bringing them
into speech about not taking (giving)
pictures. I say, *G.E.P. is: Gio is.*
And they are present.

4.

In this picture, I am a bride. I am also a daughter, sister, cousin,
in-law, niece, grandchild. A four-month fetus *is* inside of me (but
you only know because I am telling). I am dancing my first steps
as wife. A skinny man wearing a kufi and sprawling lips is
holding me. He is in my eyes. Taking me.

I burn this picture. Set afire its membranes and shadows. It *is*
no more: It *was*: We *were*.

5.

Here I speak of it,
signif it for you. Disturb,
touch it, retrace its haunt.

It is a picture again. It is.

Weaned : *Breaking the Habit of Pork*

FIRST TRIMESTER :||

No matter what I smell, it's a hot dog. And (from miles away) makes me sick. It was Andre who reminded me how meat factories take remnants from the pig, cow, or chicken and stuff them into paper-thin edible skins to make the wiener. All-American. Brand name Oscar-Meyer. Garlic and coloring, usually Red Dye No. 254 or something close to that. Boiled and stuffed in a bun, the wiener makes a nice pocket of leftovers. Remains. Food that wasn't wanted somewhere else.

SECOND TRIMESTER :||

I want it. The baby wants it. We want minced barbecue from Ralph's with coleslaw on a round bun. So I beg my husband to drive the winding mountain roads from Indianapolis to North Carolina just to get us a Ralph's barbecue sandwich. Because he loves me, he does. Eleven hours, he drives us to satisfy our craving. My mouth waters for the vinegary, red pepper hot in my mouth. But the moment I open the sandwich wrapper and the smell wafts to my nose, I am sick again. Squeamish. The thought of remnant meat from the hot dog remains. Minced pork is also a leftover stuffed into a bun. Pulled pig that was not used somewhere else.

Third trimester :||

Bloody hog killings and souse. Pork trimmings pickled, cubed, soaked in cider vinegar and chilled. Chitterlings. Pig brains and eggs. Pickled pigs' feet. Hog maws. Pork rinds. Fatback. All that is left over when the good meat is already gone. *There was a time*, my granny says, *when fatback meat was all we had. Little pork never hurt anybody at all*. I walk into the feast of swine leftovers in my mother's house. Smell makes me queasy. Odor embedding in my skin. I wash my hands insanely so that my skin will smell like skin again. But the pig remains. It Is here left over In every corner of the house. The scent of it does not linger somewhere else.

Character Language

(for my son)

Though birds and aliens
constellate to read us,
the language of hugging
has no alphabet.

Fawning limbs etched
into one another
have two component parts—
one, purpose, the other, sound.

To muffle love into rayon shoulders
or swathe it in mute cotton shirts,
human arms the smallest unit
of touch still capable of meaning.

I hug you and become interpretable,
bearing both an intimacy and distance,

an etymology of us traced
from first impression
once removed—

to the way you now
indent me.

Otherness

"I am in exile. Like everybody else, I live in a world that is given to me . . .
But it is not my native home."
      — PAUL GOODMAN, "Speaking and Language," *Defence of Poetry*, 1971

A woman I know well has stolen my face.
She answers for me when someone asks my profession:
Writer, she says, then readies our body for the certain assault.

She makes small talk with my family
about the births and deaths of old neighbors and friends
and sidesteps the cancer that licks at my mother's brain,

malignancy that waits for my own breast or bones or lungs.
The woman has died for me a thousand times,
tends the pocks and scars that come from simple breathing.

When I am in the company of black poets, she holds
my tongue. Does not protest against the suitable way
to be black enough . . . (write black enough poems).

My children adore her. She tells them stories
about how they came to be, gives them James Brown
over a plate of dirty rice, peach chutney and fried fish.

But there are days my son detects me (a front
can lie; a back always tells). He walks around the back of me
to find the face. Somewhere in the contour

of practiced muscle and grin, he discovers the brittle pupils,
cups the raised cheekbones, pulls me eye-to-his-eye,
asks the face: *Mommy, are you there?*

Fall of the House of Dora

[And now, the slaughter of the house, a snafu
of the splintered wood. The steel ball wrecks a chemistry
between preservation and memory. The zenith
of her high-breast days now gone, she sags: A Mississippi
blues on a Carolina washboard with spoons. The hip
Old Girl must die. Her belly ruptures.] Half your life becomes hypothesis:

An uncontested maybe. You can no longer test the theorem
that your grandmother can make anything delicious from leftover snafu,
In her once bright kitchen, you can't watch her drag bowlegs and a busted hip
between a sink and a wood stove to see if a dash of water sizzles, if the chemistry
of chicken fat and cast iron yields the best salted herring this side of the Mississippi.
[The back porch has come down. And with it,] the zenith

of slop buckets and corncobs for squealing hogs. (And with that) the zenith
of gingham dish towels and aluminum foot tubs bearing pea pods. There was the theory
that breakfast was best at 5 a.m. with a side of scrambled pig brains and eggs. *Mississippi
just don't get down like that*, your grandmother said, just as her son, the snafu
Uncle William, staggered through the screen door, his drunken breath a sour chemistry
of morning halitosis and ripple, his eyes more red than a rose hip.

[Glass flies, the wrecker caves the face of the house] where you with newly curved hips once sat with empty Hi-C cans and fabric at your grandmother's feet, the zenith of your learning. Footstools. Crazy quilts with no patterns. You loved the smelly chemistry of sulfur and old chimney smoke in bedcovers, over sunk-belly mattresses, the maxim being that you had a place to lay your head. You'd never make the snafu of complaining. *Because there were plenty of folks from East BoonFuck to Mississippi*

who didn't have an ounce of all your blessings. (Now Mississippi from East BoonFuck was a place you'd never been, even when you used to hop on one leg, spit in the dirt, squeeze your eyes tight, and wish for other places.) The snafu of falling face down and eating grit made you grateful, yet wanting to reach the zenith of cotton fields, a strawberry patch. To disremember your grandmother's house, to postulate on what it would be to stand short in a city landmine of buildings, to know the chemistries

of bigger places. [But this is now the biggest place you've ever known, a chemistry of your blood, the crumbling house a better find than red clay in Mississippi, lives and times that must now be left to who-said and grand hypothesis.] You will have to trust yourself to remember all the girls you've been here: hip prima donna and spunky little tomboy picking cotton. The old Zenith television still in the front room will help, if memory fails and you snafu

the facts. You remember your chemistry, that hip
memories can come at the zenith of a house dying. That Mississippi mud
has no place in Carolina. This is both hypothesis and snafu.

Clearance

Glenda Ricci's back, a bold, black hypotenuse,
cliffs in a precipice of gray cambric buttocks.
I know it's her. I've seen her gimcrack Buick,

trunk mouth open, next to the curb.
Among the grabbers—swift Lilliputians
scampering for gems—she is the one

I stare down in discernment. Past Sundays,
we'd talked teens, SAT scores, proms, spring.
She'd asked about the jonquils on the sill.

Stooping, she now fingers my first edition copy
of *The Bluest Eye*, skimming the evicted morsel
right there in the yard—cover, binding and print.

Her eyes rummage the waif of appliances,
limp shoelaces, fractured dishes, busted boxes:
torn hefty bags of homeless artifacts.

She never looks up from my ousted things.
In the grass, the spine of a shelf once mine
lies cracked. Glenda, a flank of novels,

hatches from the splinters home.

Orange

I try to tell the cashier at the Sears counter;
she puckers and continues folding the polo shirts/

a short brown woman with a clipboard and pen;
Mek we get de numbuhs. Yuh get pay, she says/

the mall cop leaned against a corner at a kiosk
guarding the gulp-size cup with a pinstripe straw/

even the little girl, plaits flying, who has fled her parents,
for the mottled show glass at The Cookie Factory,

but none of them will see him:

The wild haired man in bright orange corrections issue,
D-O-J stenciled on his back,
feet chain-cuffed, hands free,
his buck eyes little roving suns.

I see him seeing me:

a woman who has lost her goldfish,
the clear plastic temporary aquarium
punctured by my nails, falls to the floor,
bursts. The lone fish, wriggling
tail and fin in the new puddle,
is drowning in the cool air.

Boys Named Peaches

Friday: Ray up at bat in a field of weeds we've worn into a dusty diamond of cardboard bases and blades of bush-and-wild Carolina grass. In a dingy, ribbed tank that shows his disc of navel and behind the loose, raised hem where his Buddha belly moons us all, he is a peanut nebula wide enough to block cheering armpits, glee-slant eyes and bulging pubescent crotches from the sun.

field of tall secrets
blades cutting, the ankles dance:
the white pump house hums

Saturday: Ray leans back on his tubby left leg, right side of home plate, lets up a single pop, the airborne softball sending him flying bases in sandals, the straps tight between mosquito-gnawed ankles and the pink meat of his heel. A giggle of rouge, no powder puff in sight, a third coat of Holy Pink Pagoda on his left toes, Tutti Frutti Tonga on the right—a colorful lead for the fingernail Midnight in Moscow blend flailing the winning run home.

white pump house humming
boy and boy measure zippers:
snakes slide under sun

Sunday: He slips on his sister's discarded leotards and does coffee table ballet to gospel quartet hymns. His father peddles G.I. Joe in kung fu grip, no match for Lite Brite houses against black paper skies or Isis bracelets from Jewel Magic. He snags shag berber fuzz in his hair when he lands derriere against a too-tiny navy bikini on Stretch Armstrong. Elastic hugs show him how man arms become pleats for other man arms.

thigh against a thigh
a naked hand learns to grab
flies overhead buzz

Monday: Curiosity taught Ray his private, kinky hot. Boys in tube
socks. Boys in suits. Boys in school picture collars. Boys in boots.
Closed doors. Behind the well. They made him promise not to
tell. *Sissy-boy sissy.* That's what they all said. *Look at me wrong, I'll
knock you dead.* He didn't look them in the eye. Didn't tell. Boys
named Peaches: chickenshit infidels. The Peaches who filled his
mouth on Friday night. The Peaches who bent him over near
the brake light. Peaches who lied about what didn't happen in
the back rooms. Peaches who smashed the petals on his mother's
favorite blooms.

yellow flash: red sign
children load in single file
windshield: bird wing snaps

Hush Now, Don't Complain: Po' Folks' Sonnets

I.

The sonnets I know best are wrought with blues—
the sacred laughs of women through a door,
the *click clack-clack* of clunky high-heeled shoes,
and freedom that knows trouble to its core.
Where blues is sad and sonnet is a song
(both stress repeating rhythm and a rhyme),
I think it would not be at all so wrong
to call the blues a sonnet in its prime.
Complaint is delicate and genteel art:
a wailing moan says all you've not yet said.
Refrain in blues is a sonnet's patterned smarts.
To weep and whimper says you're not yet dead.

The haunt of blues is always in my head,
schemes of sonnets waiting to be read.

II.

Avon/Stratford, ain't the Serengeti.
Poet girl of *The Portuguese* is gone.
What have we to get us through regretting?
Acoustic wails in daddy's baritone.
He wang-dang-doodled right down to his bones,
and plucked the skin so raw around his thumb.
His misery was doused like cheap cologne.
His songs were just so smart they left us dumb.
There's never been a Shakespeare or a Dunne
whose lyrics had the same sweet bitter sting
as daddy's hymns of how the soul is won
or how to catch the devil with a sling.
He sang the wretched sonnets of the poor,
'til death and snatchers finally left our door.

> *Sonnet blues always calling my name.*
> *Sonnet blues always calling my name.*
> Life ain't too bad at all when you can complain.
> The verses bite and crack you up just the same.

Say-So

2004 Nov 12 pm 8 27

=POET, I believe you [stop] Mean well [stop] Do well [stop] Bring
teeth's teeth for your bite [stop] Make your ditties and dirges hum
[stop] Won't forget to play the water-filled glasses, the cowbell,
those chicken bones, [breathe] clunky kettles, the cluck roof of
your mouth, your belly or thigh [stop, stop]

Go on [stop] Gumbo ya-ya when all the scribes decide to Kum Ba
Yah [stop] Be a Poet [stop] *For real* [stop] Show your whole butt to
the stanza popes and the concrete image nuns [stop] Be magic
[stop] Realism [stop] Say you've kissed Komunyakaa and Stern
between the Pulitzer and papyrus [stop] Yep, they're both men
[stop] Point to the picture of dead Emily Dickinson as Jesus in
pincurls, a hairbreadth corset [breeze] and a satin petticoat
hoisted up to her *Lordamercy, I feel faint* kneecaps [break]

When English fails you, do this: *Imagine* [stop] Especially what
you don't know [stop] Remember the tulip is just a flower [stop]
Neat beauty [stop] Everything beneath a hot marble of sun is
music [stop] Find yours [stop] Get to the handsome twang of
decibels before there was meaning hammered into your swollen
Poet's ear [stop] Live inside every leap and bluff that is not Them
or Us who told you so [stop] Tell the tight-faced critics when they
ask that I sent you [stop] And I will send you again=

YOUR POEM,

the ars poetica/manifesto/political-persona rant

There is No Other Phrasing for *Ashy*

Pigment is wonder, awaiting its creams:
aloe, pat of Crisco, emollient Vasoline.

And ash? White forgery on a knee or shin,
water's inscriptive chiaroscuro on clean.

You know how skin tells
in an idiolect your mother understands?
(If these were clean, then *You* were clean:
ears, neck, armpits, face?)

Black skin after bathing renders
nothing literal.

For example,
when I take my time
oiling ash away,

I am saying to you
I am ashy:
My root beer-tinged elbow
is bright cinder
that burns every day.

Heritage

Or

Reasons Why At Thirty Something, A Southern
Hoodoo Celibate Biscuit-Quilting Mother Of Two,
Butternut Squash Breasted, First-Born Child Of A
Blues Farmer And A Pork Salt, Geechee-Girl Black
Bottom Princess, A Healer Full Of Belly Laughs and
Constant Light, I Am Not Whorish

my mama ain't.
her mama ain't …

though great-great
grand-great-great
granddaddy master
so-and-so
must have been.

must have been.

Part Two

I am a leader. Leaders always get heat. They're always going against the grain. Jimi Hendrix got heat; Bob Marley got heat; Miles Davis got heat. Every great artist got heat. Heat means you're doing something right.

— ZIGGY MARLEY

Burnt Cork Bop

What was going on with Marvin Gaye?
Kinda stubborn trouble man steeped in hit music,
seasoned muse brew sold like vinyl flapjacks
on turntables, chart-topping grooves.
Everybody loves a love song, but when
does anybody want the song you love?

> *Wheel about an' turn about an' do jes so,*
> *an' eb'ry time I wheel about, I jump Jim Crow.*

To write the poems that make the whole world sing!
Pat juba, dance a jig, shake some jive —
verse gives five on the black-hand side.
And what when I scribe a libretto? Or pantoum?
Or French ballade my southern fingernail moon?
Is it black enough: old lyric, new tune?
Music, they say, has social meaning, So what
does it mean if my poem's music won't shade to black?

> I'll swallow anything you want me to swallow.
> *Wheel about an' turn about an' do jes so,*
> *an' eb'ry time I wheel about, I jump Jim Crow.*

Be a better [black] poet:
Say you're Pigmeat.
Write in the custody of [black] things.
Roun' midnight, wash away your cork.
Find beneath you really are two
shades lighter than the mask.

I'm all over the page like white on rice.
I've swallowed everything you wanted me to swallow.

Wheel about an' turn about an' do jes so,
an' eb'ry time I wheel about, I jump Jim Crow.

Clay

(Joe Frazier remembers Madison Square Garden, March 8, 1971)

Red clay bruiser with nigger brag, he could dance, now,
'round Vietnam, & for his honorable divisible nation.

Clay was always Tomming somebody out. MLK was a Tom.
Jesus was a Tom, & hot sauce chitlin' swine was Tom food.

More *as-salaam alaikum* than an ex-con on a corner,
he was Cassius, pretty Ali—legend of a man.

Showed up at the gardens with his red trunks
and a mouth fulla two-fisted fight.

And me in the green trunks, facing it down,
not there to be right 'bout nothing, but in it to win.

Way I saw it, I was a man with two choices:
lose the fight or whup Clay's ass.

Couldn't go down like no sucker, either. So I battled.
11th round, it all started to run together:

Bells-grease-left jab-winner-right uppercut-loser,
a black-eyed world droning in the bloat,

his feet tapped Bojangles like soft-shoe,
blood from us both spilling Aunt Jemima red.

Josephine

"Is this a man? Is this a woman? Her lips are painted black, her skin is the color of a banana, her hair, already short, is stuck to her head as if made of caviar, her voice is high-pitched, she shakes continually and her body slithers like a snake, the sound of the orchestra seems to come from her . . ."
          — French critic, PIERRE DE REGNIER, of Josephine Baker's

                    opening night performance at the Folies-Bergère.

At 8, after St. Louis rented me
to a family of traveling musicians,
I learned to charm the palate,
please the eye, be edible,
aromatic, seedless pulp.
(*Free the senses*, I'd say;
the mind is sure to follow.)

Parisian perky shuffled along
a leaf of black bottom jazz,
I'd steal into a taverngoer's wit
while a whole room watched me.

(This they call intelligent art:)
High yella stalk,
slender and slinky,

(My bananas the best
subversive crop to mime.)

Men peeled me down
to chalky resolve
and devoured me.

Women got their fix
of fibrous calcium from me
for backbones.

Passersby slipped on this:
Juste la peau d'une femme.

(That's what I was.)

Just. Skin.

Voice Lesson from Eleanora Fagan

I.

There's a way to do this.
Sing!
& imitate yourself
when you forget the song.

Mobs of voices try
to get at you.
Mimeographing hands
want to lift your hem
& see what kind of panties
you wear.

> And who the hell is Jill Badu Scott,
> cheap red carnation in her baggage hair?

II.

Even after you die
folks still want your
signature.

Mic'd to your own life,
nothing is to scale.

Crits say *Billie in refrain*
is minimalist cuss;
her truth is
myths & wishes & lies.

But they never dragged me.
I knew to be a hive of contradictions
& drink like a man.

On the rocks and hard places,
I screwed rogue-daddy lovers
down to the white meat.

I was bourbon dark
& straight razor bright.

Super Freak

(The Ballad of Rick James: 2.1.48–8.6.04)

She's a very kinky girl, the kind you don't take home to mother.
She's a very kinky mother, and your heart won't hold the girl.
She's a kinky very super freaky, cocky mynah bird.
And wherever you can find her, you find love.

In my world, a habit cost seven thousand dollars a week,
hustle & hassle rebel causes that looped me wild.
I was crackerjack of the curly wig erotic,
and where there wasn't crimp grease falling
on black leather shoulders, there was dope sweat
from the thick squeegee of hair
needling through my honeycomb scalp.

How it is I came to the hotel room,
the sizzling pipe and trick woman both in hand,
how she turned for me in that hour,
how purple/black/blue daisies were bustin'
out under her skin, how it wasn't me
(I never hit her), how I always got fucked.
It's not exactly a trick mystery. It's way
more bare-bones than that:
I was always Rick James, bitch,
and I loved what I loved.

He's a Main Line punk funk icon with his braids flung over shoulder.
He is Slick James Johnson Jr., joined the Navy at fifteen.
And his mama was a maid who ran the numbers for a dime,
a Hail Mary tossed when she could find the time.

I've seen bars. At least twice.
More if you count the windows in my house,
sometimes covered with aluminum foil.
Nothing could keep me when the music of the funk called.
The Navy tried, but I went AWOL.
The inner freak in me wanted to be out.
(Room 714, always waiting.)
Any white alkaloid could take me by the nostrils,
but it took a funky chord to take me by the nose.

The rap cats forever wanted to sample me.
Late 80s fancy dance gold-rimmed glasses,
ballooned genie pants and *oh-oh-oh-oh,*
ohoh-oh-oh (I touched that).
A conversion, the epiphany, and royalties later,
I still got bank, and he is a man of God.
Will *Jiggy Wit' It Smith*, LL Cool James,
or Mary J. *Love Without a Limit*—all needed samples,
to get broke off a piece of my bronze thigh funk,
get some *Blow, Danny* for their shoestring songs.

In the morning August 6, his heart did its last open-shutter.
In the morning August 6, his fire-desire went stone cold blood.
Found him in his bed, Rick James was dead, his funk-n-roll was done.
As for Super Freaks, there'll always be just one.

---

* Italicized stanzas are to be sung to an operatic tune created by the poet.

Part Three

We must rather conclude from this that heat itself is a motion, an internal invisible motion of the smallest elementary particles of bodies.

— HERMANN VON HELMHOLTZ

Where it is a duty to worship the sun it is pretty sure to be a crime to examine the laws of heat.

— JOHN MORLEY

News of the weird : Penis roams MARTA train

ATLANTA—Today on MARTA, the city's public
transit system, a brown penis poked out from
a young thug's open fly.

Authorities say the unnamed genitals belonged to
a black man in his early twenties wearing braids
and a white wife beater.

As the train left the Five Points station heading
south toward Hartsfield-Jackson International
Airport, the penis bunted its head between
the rungs of a gold zipper.

Commuters continued to read books and news-
papers as the penis stretched out of the young
man's fatigue pants and bobbed to onlookers.

"I can't believe they just kept reading those books
like tarot cards," said Cruzita Gomez. "How could you
not pay attention to a *pene—bolas*—on the loose?"

Gomez and her sister Ana were the first to spot
the roving muscle and flesh. The two erupted
in laughter while speaking Spanish.

"I always heard about these. So big. Now I've seen
with my own eyes," Ana said.

Other passengers say the young man realized
his penis was the subject of gawking and laughter
when the train stopped at the East Point station.
He felt an inrush of air when the doors opened
to release riders.

The young man immediately zipped his pants,
flashed a look at other patrons, uttered words
in Spanish to the Gomez sisters and dashed
off the train.

According to MARTA officials, the scene marks
the first time paying customers have had to watch
an unescorted body part move independent
of its owner.

Cherryl Floyd-Miller, who was traveling to The Cheese-
cake Factory to pick up an order for her downtown
office at the time, described the penis as beautiful.

"Gorgeous. Art, pure art. It's time to retire the Statue
of David from my memory forever," she said. "I've
never seen a ding-a-ling that flawless."

In an effort to allay the fears of regular customers,
and prevent future occurrences, MARTA wants to talk
to the man and investigate the incident. Police do not
intend to file any charges.

Based on data from the Institute for Sexual Habits, 87 percent of men in social settings do not know when their fly is open in public. Ninety-eight percent of those men: black.

Though sketches of the man based on descriptions by passengers on the train have been circulated throughout the city, neither the man nor his penis had been identified at the time of this report.

Darfur

"They were young when time was heavy
where they came from,
and precious seconds lingered
as though their last ones."

           — from the song "History" by JULIA BIEL

The necklace of sheeny Janjaweed bullets: *Mene ne Yake faruwa?*
He does not remove them as he cleaves Mummy: *Me ka ke so?*
Four legs, a *blokkus*, one middle gash, one bushel of arms.
Komene ne ya ke yi ba shi da kyau. Overhead, hard white gas
and the squeal of metal birds, their bellies full of unsalted ransom.
Mummy's open *bobbi* Janja-wet. The birds' worms will miss my tongue.

     Far away from where they started came their children,
     And all the things they'd suffered, they kept well-hidden.

Boju-Boju. Yellow. *Dey come again o!* Water measured
by the slippery, bright capful for my houseless family of twelve.
I am the smallest and drink first. One warm swallow trickling
past barbed ribs. I do not care that the gnat on my lash & lids
has tried to take a sip. I am inside my mind, memorizing aromas
of flesh. Fire, tin, rancid squirrelfish: That is the smell of the dead.
Sweat, musk, sand, semen: This, the scent of the Janjaweed.
We who still live? *Dorti-dorti*, paper bodies waiting for any small wind.

And all the things they'd suffered, they kept well-hidden.
They felt as safe as houses in their new prison.

There is no *fada* here. No father tongue. No *fada* hands.
No laughing Dinka danshiki waving invisible spears between crooked
poles on drooping laundry lines. Swollen women are starved for home.
There is the Janjaweed's dusty hand ripping again at Mummy's george,
I draw my throat, bent for a gworo from my phantom *fada's* hands,
I am becoming the Janjaweed, a spore of dead eyes in a dervish of guns.

They fall to ash like houses in Darfur prisons.
But history lives on children's faces, so what can protect them?
What? What? What can protect them?

Souvenirs

Who doesn't know better?
Who thinks there is worse?
Who slips the knot into noose to get first say?
Who'll snatch the body from its night-night and prey?
Who lifts the head-top to the tree-arm?
What snaps the neck? Who does first harm?

Someone take a finger.
Someone take a toe.
Someone take the cooked flesh.
When he hollers, don't let go.

Not enough? Want more? Go to his mama's front door.
Rip the roof, rock the window—anything to wage the war.
Find the herniated guilt of corroded navel skin,
kept for keeps and keeping kept in old funk-hole juju gin.
Find the rag, a sugartit, where he cut his first small teeth
in the re-used pig skin bag, stashed like all his mama's grief,
and the crooked-lip love letter that set off all this hell bent rage,
clean and Anglo, girl's cherry kiss, smeared so floozie on the page.

Have yourself a tooth.
Get yourself a nail.
Take yourself an eyeball.
Send him straight to hell.

Noosed, juiced, and now he's reduced
to hung, and dumb, dead and warned.
Who takes the picture of a limp dick in a tree?
Who writes the headline? Who cuts the body free?
Who said this was used-to-be? Who said nevermore?
Who did it in 1960? Who in 2004?

Someone flash the bulb.
Someone snap the flash.
Someone set a fire,
turn a man to ash.

Stowaway the father.
Batten down the son.
Steal away to Jesus . . .
don't forget your gun.

Skunk

*"What I'm hearing, which is sort of scary, is they all want to stay in Texas.
(Said with concern.) . . . so many of the peoples in the arena here, you know,
they're underprivileged anyway, so this—this (she chuckles slightly) is
working very well for them."*

— BARBARA BUSH

She thought of roux (what else to do?),
A clot of trouble in her face,
A yank of white and blue-eyed blue,

A blather of words—loose-phlegm flew.
Good heartland crust, off-Dixie taste,
What could she do but think of roux,

Give The Big Easy its proper due?
An aftermath would shrink (efface
in yanks of white and blueblood blue)

The winded stench. What else to do,
Kennebunkport charm and Texas grace?
In this death hour, she thought of roux

And how these bodies in their stew
Became our cataclysmic nation's waste.
Miss Yank of White, Miss Spat of Blue,

What had she really come to do,
Ration the exodus, water? Give face?
She bilked the cameras, made social roux,
Her yank of white, its blue-eyed blue.

Heats

Times the flesh
conspires to burn,
smoldering your most recent lives
into your next.

Times the body—
as anchored kite,
as tender snatch of warmth—
will stream.

In some animals,
a show of teeth
is aggression,
revving before the lunge.

Times we primates come
all teeth in the fender
and roaring:
Carbon casing giving
hiss, sizzle and foam.

What are we when we're gone?
The molecule? Missing spleen
and present bone?
Shells sucked clean
of liver and pearl?

Times we genuflect to memory,
become red-eye wave and gesture,

are flickers on the eyeball,

exquisite recurring heats.

Part Four

I don't always wear underwear. When I'm in the heat, especially, I can't wear it. Like, if I'm wearing a flower dress, why do I have to wear underwear?

— NAOMI CAMPBELL

Night Is Given

"... feeling that sunlight is/(life and day are) only loaned :whereas/night is given (night and death and rain/are given; . . ."

— EE CUMMINGS, "Now I by (with everywhere around),"
from 73 *Poems*

A.

night. named. descends. declension.

thirty. conjugate. griefs.

lay. open. as-if. treasons.

devil's. got. rag. dolls.

darned. remnants. sutured. sin.

nights. dowry. is. given.

days. blades. sorrow. lends.

B.

night.   descends.

    thirty.   griefs.

open.   treasons.

        devil's. rag.

    remnant.   nights.

given.   sorrow.

        lends.

Unknuckled

I am not at the busted white plaster,
at his fist print in a broken wall.

I am not sitting vigil
for his amnesiac trigger finger,
not pressing fast tears
against a cold rifle barrel.

He is not gazing at his hands
as if they belong
to some other man.

He is not saying, "Someone's
gonna die tonight,"
and leaving.

He is not at an Elkhart hotel
with the second woman
on the night I discover
the first.

We are not debating
how she got our number.

On the days he makes it
for dinner, there is not a tidy table
where I host his chatter
with our children.

I am not the steam from skillet cabbage,
not the cast iron pan resting
on the stove's black eye.

We are not days deep in silence.

We are not entering
the months of absence,
abstinence.

We are not sleeping
back to back.

We have not parted our lives.

We are at an altar, promising
to be token and fire.

A man with a legal Bible
and an Indiana love edict
is asking us
if we will . . . until,

and we are saying yes,
for life.

The Beautiful, Needful Thing

(after Robert Hayden)

In love, there are heights where air, necessary
breadth, approaches need. No reprieve for you there.

Just before he says goodbye, his interloping arms
a crooked sprawl tangential to your shoulder mass,

he tells you what a moon you are: He is a yearner,
though you are a lifespan out of reach. He burns away.

This is your *free*; an episodic heat with him is done.
But morning comes, exacting its articulate mums.

Then night again when air hangs like a body. Hopeful
ecliptic dog star, you notice lovesick chirps of crickets.

You wait in your sky for glints of lightning bugs,
pray to a galaxy goddess to banish liberty from *need*.

Burgeon

You used to open for me, didn't you? At four o'clock in the middle of the afternoon
or in the middle of the night. You and the lovely would come, bright, lush.
Instant. A spread of wild oats. I knew how to touch you then. Knew
which spot was *the* spot. It changed every single time, and I
always found it. I could not wait to find the daisy
in the middle of your back, the dahlias
I could make bud from the backs
of your knees. How you could
come to me with the hard
world under your skin
and let me
rub it
all
away.
You cottoned
to me. Every single time.
But now I'm the hard world to you,
a hedge of devil's flax and thorns. I just can't
touch you anymore. In the places where you would move
for me, run to me, river for me, you are weeds. And you act

like there is a stigma attached to wanting me. Like *you* can't come
to me anymore. Think I'd asked you stop breathing or something. I have waited
for months, and nothing. Not a single bell rings when you look at me. You don't move.
Not a vein. Not a sprig. Everything is tight. Tell me: How can a woman so closed ever *flower?*

Something called a wife-beater

should pulse and whisk,
miscegenate the yolk
of woman's vixen wile
into marriage.

His just hugged. Dingy
ribbed, sleeveless tee
burgeoning new arm bulk
curled from shoulders,
suspending fists—

an eggshell knuckle
of cotton near the armpit
moaning for bleach.

Defecting: A Bop for Exit Signs

Away. In rock shoulders. Rambling mountain
roads have corners. These things I work to remember:
Wild billy goat with lopsided mouth of earth and weed;
in a field, a rusted water pump; cotton; white sun; static
of the tires turning against the road. This to forget: The voices
we put on at home here with me in the car.

I'll be a bag of bones driving down the road alone.

I could turn back? Yield the distance I've come to leave you
where you are. Taste more whiskey in your kisses. Be ugly
and in love again? Three wooden crosses every twenty miles.
Has somebody died for me? Eighteen-wheeler rigs clawing
five-degree inclines. Emergency exit ramps. Water springs
from the rock. Our silver up for hock. The signs: Peach cider
and bargain fireworks. Everything—anything—sells.

I waited 'til I saw the sun. I don't know why I didn't come.

I might miss your shameless flowers. Gaga gazing. Knowing
with my eyes closed where you are. Now I have no special
place to be. The road always makes me run. Days and half
the nights are my own. A stranger's in my car alone,
tuning the radio for music. Any old song will do. I'm a
          hundred
miles from home.

Something has to make you run. I don't know why I didn't come.
Don't know why I didn't come.

---

* Italicized repetitions are a refrain from Nora Jones's "Don't Know Why."

Elimination Art

Could be love ~~is in the~~ details,
~~affection and solicitude~~ reduce
to why ~~we ever come to be in love,~~
~~adore a~~ dearest ~~singular into mate,~~
~~at ever~~ all.

~~What~~ moves us ~~beyond crush,~~
~~past crunching an Other down~~
into ~~a sole~~ fit,

~~over the fringe of~~ doting
on ~~an Other's flange of nose,~~
~~crimp of fingers, chiasma of~~
~~brawn and~~ bone:

~~Is~~ devotion~~, fidelity to~~
~~an Other's~~ alters,
~~the ail and constancy of~~ becoming:

~~Minutia of dirty socks,~~
~~long-term random access memory,~~
unashamed ~~farting,~~
~~a cold foot touching for~~ warmths
~~on cold sheets —~~

~~love, the love child of habit~~
~~and~~ whimsical need.

Cum Tender

Blessing for the hard ex-

The kind of tender—
disembodied—

that could turn
our salt to sugar,

could dimple
crisp fitted sheets,

and when re/coming,
could be the elegant onset

of used mattress sag,
make you arc your backbone

to catch each hot, dirty
secret I could gurgle

through sweat—*ohhh*
and *oooh*

that feverish tender
you owned

in the holy hours
of first woo,

while the ghosts
of our breath

loaned their first
two-faced promises

in the blind
but surefooted press

of involved skin,
yesss,

that kind of tender,
may it come in you again,

in every pore of your skin
a gingery clove scaling,

may it bloom
in the tally of hard regret

you nasty off to me now,
in this, the bitter scrap

of your *ordinary* life
without me.

Childless, An Abridged Blues

Man who took my children always said he never would.
Say the man who took my children always said he never would.
But a man will say a thousand things when the *gimme-some* is good.

A yippee-dog was howling when he laid me on my back
Oh a yippee-dog was howling when he spread me on my back.
Felt the pillows wheeze and give, knocked the bed right off its slats.

My spine stretched like a ladder from my tailbone to my neck
My little spine rung like a ladder; he climbed my tailbone to my neck
If I was a car that he could drive, we'd veer off the road and wreck.

First time he was late for dinner, called me nicely on the phone.
First time late-for-supper sinner called me nicely on the phone.
When I called him back at midnight, I heard a hussy voice just groan.

Packed my bags and quit that man, took my kids and headed South.
Glad ragged, I went and quit that man, took my kids and headed South.
By then I couldn't believe a word that came out his no-good mouth.

He took the kids for early Christmas. Said he'd see me when they got back.
Drove down to get them for Christmas. Grinned his words, molasses black.
Two weeks late, my temper gone, police cars couldn't hold me back.

Man sued me for custody, ran me low-down, dragged my name.
That fool sued me for custody, low-down *nummuts* dragged my name.
Brought that groaning girl to testify. Hussy didn't have no shame.

People tried to feed me Jesus cause they thought I wanted to die.
Came all holy and prestigious cause they thought that I might die.
Told me saints were made to suffer, but they couldn't tell me why.

When a man can take your children after saying that he won't,
When his hands can snatch your children while his mouth says he won't,
Scrawl his words in blood with a butcher knife. Might be childless if you don't.

[66]

Part Five

When the water starts boiling it is foolish to turn off the heat.
~Nelson Mandela

Jo Ha Kyu

panorama, hopscotch
face in a crowd, here then gone
butterscotch, spring

a wink and a nod
early morning petal beads
prickly heat, dew

two sets of brown eyes
focus, aperture, quick flash
undulating sun

infatuation:
dry mouth, smothering air
just before the breeze

fingers chafe flesh
splayed hands digging spiky hair
midnight: tapered, lit

here and there and there
finger imprints gone too soon
night fizzles, full moon

empty bed, white sheets
how to preserve the scent of you?
dive to sheet white snow

Seersucker

An open lip of silk
ratting out the vanished button,
his shirt a linen pellicle
sheathing me in all his smells—
Gaultier fragrance at the collar,
lemony starch on either sleeve,
bare-bottom me under his threads,
an ether of fresh sweat.

At times I'm in his boxers,
for brawny thickets of his thighs,
(notice the toothbrush holder
where he's left a space for me)
or slosh in his timber boots—
for quick dashes to my car.

                    I love
his sundry things,
worn garments he's shed,

flagrant love
when he shirts me,
stitch, striping and seam.

In Another Life, A Bluesman

Or maybe a dredloc'd shaman,
your chickenfoot Peetie Wheatstraw gospel

bigger than some cliché amulet tucked in a blood-
stained pouch. Or maybe a birth doula

whose distinct blend of tree root
and blue cohosh coaxed the most

stubborn infants out of their mothers
into their own large lives. If you

were either of those—life priest
or deliverer—I wz yr con'jr dust

or your knotted life-making hands.
But if (for true) you were a bluesman,

then we leaned into each other,
me into Everything, you into All.

I wz the quiver in your midriff
while you delivered the hard luck story,

its comeuppance, a faithful wit.
I wz the dog-whistle scream that chased

your red-earth squall. I wz
your bittersweet, liver-deep lick.

Somewhere in the snarl of rot-gut whiskey
rasp buoying up through your windpipe

and the incantatory washboard moan—
some/time when the blues became the way

a man who filled with flatted thirds
could heist the world onto the width

of a snagnail and keep it spinning,
you and I, *Bluesman*, made words

hot like mercury boil the air.
We were the reason

folks in a washed out delta
could still have a fetish with a song.

Salamander

Hetero fear between us
a flimsy line you won't cross,

I hiss. Move nocturnal.
Wrap my pincer toes
around a chinaberry tree,
Hang upside down. Hide.

My glass skin, grown spiny
from your compliment, beads
with connotation. I want to bathe
in the scent of lime verbena,
rinse my cold blood in moonlight,
red-salmon orange.

A fire-bellied newt,
I burrow in any crevice we could invent
among the hard bloom of igneous rock.
I inflate my defenseless body, dare you
to find me in the dark, dank memory
of a lust cycle.

When you bring these soft words to me,
I smother the urge to squirt blood
from my eye sockets,
show an impressive dewlap
of matted hair.

My cryptic throat fan colors—
or the Madagascan blue tail I've grown
waiting for you to come unafraid—
shame the day sky-fried white.

In the dire places
where I've made sanctuary,
I resort to my secretive habits,
fake my own death
perched on a bromeliad leaf.

I camouflage when you are near,
tuck myself into all
the unconditional clauses of your life,
laugh and conspire this ease with you,
deceive your cunning, rambling eye.

Rhythm Method

           To blow,
inhale you in flashes,
tiptoe a landmine of grunts,
deaf, dumb breathing—

           kisses
tell your new music,
traipse and moan
your catacomb's cavernous
changing patterns.

Hips warble elegies
for the thousand
spasmodic strangers.
you were before now.

How did *we* move
the first time?

Callow humping?
Slow, restrained
spin-top swirls?

Or open and go,

and gone?

Love Case Study No. 12

Neck-to-ankle adorned in hip denim, he has
a measured, cool stance. Middle-aged American male.
Divorced at least twice. Loved at least once.
His eyes in a stupor, the intermittent panic in them
darting behind the lenses of ocher specs.
He is the Poet, proper noun. His sovereignty
waving from the roots of his fab hair.
We have come on the winds of book prize celebrity
to hear his words.

He takes a seat. Crosses and uncrosses
at intervals, his legs. He shifts, unaffected,
unaffectionate. The bobbed, bubbly blonde
at his side who smiles unashamed sex sheen,
pulls his arm to tug him closer. A red shirt
over slight breasts and a not quite cadaverous
chassis of bones, (slim jeans, brown pumps
and toffee brittle body wafture to match).
She does not suspect that we have known him
in a previous life. *Then he loved a woman*
half his body but twice his size,
a woman who imported war-torn countries
through her eyes, the upturned corners of her smile
always the small, erupting birthplace
of a distant, unnamed star. She is more present
in his frequented places when she is nowhere
to be found. An absence (the light of her,
the winks of love she hastened in him)
now becomes a spot of light he can grow grizzly in.

Finally his turn at the mic, he reads an ornery poem
that is a curse. It tumbles from his mouth, a bouquet
of switchblades scattered on the concrete floor
around our simple, metal folding chairs.
In a language more acrid than salt, more steady
than death, he wishes someone's daughter love,
a hex he believes will miss his own daughter.

He wrote more tender poems in his foregone lives,
the one just before Bitter, the one just after Trust.

He returns to his seat. Settles back
into the effervescing blonde. She is not paying
attention to her own feet. *He is all that matters.*
Her heel kicks over a plastic cup of red wine
left beneath her chair. The wine bitches
into a puddle disgorging over the lip
of the cup like fresh blood.

Churn

Giggles over pasta.

Side glances through
leather declaratives,
(your *never,* my *not* and *absolutely not*)
the loves we will not love again.

> Auld Lang Syne raises her bitter sickle
> against our forgetting trysts
> that have brought us
> to whatever *this*
> is this.

I speak of men I've known
as curds of butterfat
put to some other use—
the sour breath of memory over
sweet acidophilus tongue.

> You separate me
> from your other girl,
> the one who was my height,
> thick and lowdown feisty,
> (but who could *never*
> have written this poem).

> In a barely black room,
> as we diphthong limbs
> into new language,

we nest in gallons of
of sheets and walls,
churn Coltrane into gouda,
taste bud, navel and lobe.

Unafraid of our dark,
we match tentacle fingers.
Body eddies body into curves.

Snake Oil

Clear water in the glass could be vodka or halcyon snake oil.
Hear daughter, the thud of chokecherries landing in rococo snake oil.

He squats on frangipani, croaks of three lids rubbed in Geechee salt.
Washed in deep river holy water, his teeth are polished with snake oil.

Hot memories slither cheeky to the schmooze bone. *Run-run. Skip. Run.*
What's got us now for dinner? Tilapia bone talisman dipped in snake oil?

He catches me by the tongue, my uvula bathed in his taste buds.
He unplugs my holler note, *besa mis dobleces* with snake oil.

Cock the Rooster watches from a corner as we swallow each other's words.
My feet have been his mother's. She cooks everything from scratch in snake oil.

His grandmother is in the lava lamp whose oil and water don't mix.
We heat. Green liquid bellies roll adagio through lemon chiffon snake oil.

We alcatraz to Marley bop and Badu, a spicy, speaker-blast scat
Tight in my thighs, a tissue burns. He rouses the flame with snake oil.

As he presses his breath into my face, I remember three other imagined times.
My Beloved is the Dog Star conjuring a whispery night sky with his snake oil.

You know my name: Cherryl: ecstatic ache: warbling thunder in a moonstorm.
Break me open like pomegranate; ripe flesh is bright seed in snake oil.

Afterspotting

flat needle on E, the rancid sun drench rotting the dashboard
an almost greasy windshield conjuring pork rinds, old cracklin'
skin. overexposed neckfat. i am empty with sweat. the mouth
of a river has opened and screams out of me. at the bend of
my fifth cramp, i begin to name the trees: Ezekiel (no middle
name). or a girl: Ella Bijoux. i push harder. more gas. more fat.
all blood.

push. name the blood Ezekiel at the middle of my fifth cramp.
i am all windshield sun. almost girl greasy. more rancid. i needle
the dashboard on E. no. gas. the flat rotting. screams. i begin
to name a river of pork skin Ella Bijoux. or neckfat. the fat, empty
mouth has opened. and overexposed the rinds of trees. an out:
a harder drench, more cracklin' gut. the conjuring bend. sweat.

Voodoo Chicken

Gots me hanker. Gots me squall, peeping tall-Tom
at your lovely, in your throat, and the itch,
hellcat itch, of it rides me like a witch
into the nights, those crafty nights, no calm
will come. You just a mule teeth puppet show.
Stop and go. Chickenhearted to the core.
you say don't cross the line or crack the door.
How sweetmeat, milk. How navy black. How crow.

But love has stayed and love is made, is *all*
is *with*, *for*. We almost did, just about,
said we (*nohow*) wouldn't (*nungh-ungh*) fall.
This moot jinx so far in, it's inside out.
We say we won't. But reckon do. Yak. Stall
for *if*. Wait for good-good. Gut in. Ass out.

Celie in Atlanta

dearGod,

Shug be a man now.
She got raspy chest hair and grunt.
Every time my shug be on the phone to X,
croonin' low buzz and lovely whir,
I be boilin' grits, over butane
clangin' butter in spoons.

Printed in the United Kingdom
by Lightning Source UK Ltd.
136438UK00001B/256-354/P